30 Days of Joyful Meditation

30 Days of Joyful Meditation

Take the Journey

Pam Ross

Pam Ross
KLD Publishing, USA
2018

30 Days of Joyful Meditation Copyright © 2018 Pam Ross All rights reserved. This book or any portion thereof may not be reproduced or used in any manner whatsoever without the express written permission of the publisher except for the use of brief quotations.

Unless otherwise noted,
"Scripture quotations taken from the Amplified® Bible (AMP), Copyright © 2015 by The Lockman Foundation Used by permission. www.Lockman.org"

Printed by Create Space, Inc in the United States of America.

First printing, 2018
KLD Publishing
2158 45 th St. #350
Highland, IN, 46322
www.pamross.com
ISBN: -13: 978-1-7325778-1-7

First Edition: July 2018

10 9 8 7 6 5 4 3 2 1

DEDICATION

To all who will take the journey and to my children, Imani, Nia and Zoe. I couldn't ask for better people to take this journey with me.

Remember, joy is for the strong.

CONTENTS

DEDICATION..V
CONTENTS...VII
INTRODUCTION..IX
HEAVEN REJOICED OVER YOU.......................1
THE KINGDOM'S DOOR IS CHILD SIZED.........3
YOUR JOY RESTORED....................................5
BEST SEAT IN THE HOUSE..............................7
HELL, NO!..9
DRIVE YOUR MIND.......................................11
RELATIONSHIP CAPITAL................................13
WILD JOY...15
A REASON TO REJOICE................................17
SET OVER MUCH..19
ENDURING JOY..21
MORNING JOY...23
HEALED, DELIVERED AND SET FREE............25
DIG ANOTHER WELL....................................27
ABOUNDING JOY..29
ALWAYS BE JOYFUL.....................................31

SHOUTS OF JOY	33
OUR DAILY JOY	35
LOST IN TRANSLATION	37
WORK WITH JOY	39
CONTROL + "S"	41
NO MATTER WHAT	43
SON OF ENCOURAGEMENT	45
SET YOUR MIND	47
FROM LABOR TO JOY	49
RECONCILED TO JOY	51
SOLD OUT TO JOY	53
A JOYFUL FUTURE	55
JOY MD	57
FOREVER JOYFUL	59

Introduction

Your Brain on Joy

Much of our brain activity is automatic. That's why we can drive home from work the same way every day without giving it a single thought. Unfortunately for most people, much of that automatic brain activity is also harmful. Double Board-Certified Psychiatrist and Neuroscientist Dr. Daniel Amen coined the term, Automatic Negative Thoughts (ANTs). You should know that these ANTs affect your mind and body.

> 2 Corinthians 10:5 Casting down imaginations, and every high thing that exalteth itself against the knowledge of God, and bringing into captivity every thought to the obedience of Christ.

Negative pathways are created in the brain when we fail to "cast down" dark thoughts. In short, the ANTs move in. Eventually, we won't feel the joy around us even when good things happen. Have you ever wondered why you didn't feel happy when you should?

According to cognitive neuroscientist, Dr. Caroline Leaf, anti-depressant medications numb the brain so that we feel less darkness. They do not create positive pathways. Thankfully, God created us with the ability to change our brain. Thoughts are both physical and dynamic; they move and change. This process is called neuroplasticity. Meditating on the word of God creates new pathways, killing those ANTs and empowering us to live the life God has for us.

Why Meditation?

> Joshua 1:8 This Book of the Law shall not depart from your mouth, but you shall read [and meditate on] it day and night, so that you may be careful to do [everything] in accordance with all that is written in it; for then you will make your way prosperous, and then you will be [a]successful.

Meditation means to mull things over in your mind. One of the translations of the word meditate is to chew. Chewing our food well, allows us to get the most nutrition out of it and digest it well. Meditating on the truth of God's word will enable us to get the most out of what we read and apply it to our lives. Anything else is religious activity and a waste of time.

Romans 12:2 And do not be conformed to this world [any longer with its superficial values and customs] but be [a]transformed and progressively changed [as you mature spiritually] by the renewing of your mind *[focusing on godly values and ethical attitudes], so that you may prove [for yourselves] what the will of God is, that which is good and acceptable and perfect [in His plan and purpose for you].*

Let's face it, the world around us is distracted, pessimistic and void of real hope. We were born in and to this cynical world, but Romans12:2 teaches us how to be transformed. Real change happens as your mind is renewed. Only the word of God can make your mind new.

Renewing your mind involves your will; you must be willing to change. Notice the Amplified Bible translation explains this process as "focusing." However, it is not solely an act of the will. It is imperative that you partner with God and follow His leading on this journey to greater joy. Your relationship with Jesus will give you the power to BE different, not just do things differently for 30 days.

> 2 Corinthians 5:17 Therefore if any man be in Christ, he is a new creature: old things are passed away; behold, all things are become new.

Take a minute to answer each of these questions honestly. Are you in Christ? How is your relationship with Jesus compared to your closest friend? How is the level of intimacy and honesty in your communication with Him? How well do you recognize God's voice in your heart? Are you quick and comfortable following His leading? Have you said or done things that put distance between you and God?

Pray this prayer to renew your connection with God.

Father God, I recognize that I have sinned against you. I confess my sins and ask that you forgive me and wash me clean from anything that would put distance between us. I believe that Jesus willingly died for my sins; He rose from the dead and is alive with you in Heaven. I receive Jesus as my Savior. I ask that you fill me with your Holy Spirit and empower me to live a life of righteousness, peace, and joy'. Amen!

Congratulations! Now you're ready to take this journey hand in hand with your Heavenly Father.

This guide is organized in three parts.

READ IT. Meditate on what God is saying to you about regaining, enriching or expanding your joy. Commit to reading the scripture of the day at least twice a day.

WEAR IT. Here's where it gets personal. Custom fit the word of the day to your life. Ask God questions. Yes, He still speaks to the hearts of His people. Record your thoughts. It's important that you are brutally honest with yourself. Take responsibility for your joy. Make no excuses. God will help you make the needed changes but only if you're honest with Him.

SHARE IT. Give the gift of joy! Revelation is demonstrated in relationships. Each day contains instructions for being a force of joy in your world. Share the joy in words or actions. You can also journal your experience at the end of each day.

Field Guide: Tips for Navigating the Real World.

- Be consistent. If you miss a day pick it up the next day. Don't get religious and start "checking the boxes." Your focus is not on finishing but on changing. If you get to the end of a day and can't recall your joy focus, you may want to repeat that day.

- Be aware. If your normal has been negative, living joyfully will feel odd, unnatural or maybe even silly. Remember normal is for the weak, joy is for the strong.

- Be resolved. Don't quit. Remember, what we learned in the book portion. Real change requires a revelation, a role model, a regimen and a righteous resolve. Be resolved to building an unstoppable you.

- Be intentional. Remember why you started this journey of joy. Take a moment and write down ways JOY will improve your life. When you begin to wonder, "why am I doing this," refer to your list and keep going. You can do this. God is with you every step of the way.

30 DAYS OF JOYFUL MEDITATION

Day 1

Heaven Rejoiced Over You

Luke 15:8 "Or what woman, if she has ten silver coins [each one equal to a day's wages] and loses one coin, does not light a lamp and sweep the house and search carefully until she finds it? **9** And when she has found it, she calls together her [women] friends and neighbors, saying, 'Rejoice with me, because I found the lost coin!' **10** *In the same way, I tell you, there is joy in the presence of the angels of God over one sinner who repents* [that is, changes his inner self—his old way of thinking, regrets past sins, lives his life in a way that proves repentance; and seeks God's purpose for his life]." (Emphasis added)

Regardless of how you came into the Kingdom, Heaven rejoiced over you! Can you relate to the woman who found the coin in Luke 15? In her search, she cleaned her house, sweeping away dirt and turning on lights until, at last, she found it. Just like that coin was in the house, the joy of the Lord is in you, waiting to be uncovered. Are you willing to sweep away some dirt and turn on some lights? Ask God which three areas of your life He wants to be swept clean and filled with light as you recover your greater JOY. Write them below.

1) My Desire to ~~serve~~ Serve people
2) Living Out Loud Unapologetically
3) Temper

Gift of gift of prayer. Tell someone that you are on a journey of JOY. Ask them to pray with you as God is increasing you in this area. Pray for their joy as well. Agree to check-in with them in 30 days.

Day 2

The Kingdom's Door is Child Sized

Matthew 18:1 At that time the disciples came to Jesus and asked, "Who is greatest in the kingdom of heaven?" **2** He called a little child and set him before them, **3** and said, "I assure you *and* most solemnly say to you, unless you repent [that is, change your inner self—your old way of thinking, live changed lives] and become like children [trusting, humble, and forgiving], you will never enter the kingdom of heaven.

The movie "Charlie and the Chocolate Factory" tells the story of poverty-stricken Charlie Bucket who finds a golden ticket that grants him a tour of Willy Wonka's Chocolate Factory, the most wonderful place in the world. To enter the factory, Charlie, along with four other children and their adult chaperones, must pass through a tiny door. The children are eager to enter, but the adults doubt they could ever fit. The little door opens a great door that leads to "a world of pure imagination." Ask God how you can be more trusting, humble, and forgiving to access more of the Kingdom of JOY. Write your thoughts below.

_____
_____
_____
_____
_____
_____
_____
_____

Give the gift of fun! Choose one of the following ways to have some child-like fun. Play your favorite childhood game. Host a game night with friends. Turn lunchtime into playtime and challenge a coworker to your favorite game.

Day 3

Your Joy Restored

Psalm 51:10-12 Create in me a clean heart, O God, And renew a right *and* steadfast spirit within me. Do not cast me away from Your presence. And do not take Your Holy Spirit from me. 12 Restore to me the joy of Your salvation And sustain me with a willing spirit.

Repentance, the ability to change your mind and ways, is one of the greatest technologies available to us as Kingdom citizens. Without repentance, we will never transform, we will never reach our potential, and we will never fulfill our destinies. True repentance leads to joy because it brings us closer to God. Spend some time praying the words of Jesus in Matthew 6:12, "And forgive us our debts, as we forgive our debtors." How does knowing you are forgiven bring you joy? Write your thoughts.

 Give the gift of reconciliation. Is there anyone to whom you need to apologize? Reach out to them today and offer an apology. Be debt free.

Day 4

Best Seat in the House

Ephesians 2:4 But God, who is rich in mercy, because of His great love with which He loved us, **5** even when we were dead in trespasses, made us alive together with Christ (by grace you have been saved), **6** and raised *us* up together, and made *us* sit together in the heavenly *places* in Christ Jesus.

Life's problems can seem so big that you feel small in comparison. Thankfully, you have been made alive with possibilities. You have been raised from defeat. You are seated with Christ in Heavenly places and things look a lot different from up there. Ask God to help you see a challenge or circumstance from Heaven's perspective. How does His perspective differ from yours? How does this make you feel? Write your thoughts here.

---

30 DAYS OF JOYFUL MEDITATION

 Give the gift of grace and mercy. Be gracious and merciful to someone by giving them something they didn't earn and may not deserve.

Day 5

Hell, No!

Psalm 16:10 For thou wilt not leave my soul in hell; neither wilt thou suffer thine Holy One to see corruption. 11 You make known to me the path of life; in your presence there is fullness of joy; at your right hand are pleasures forevermore.

Hell is anywhere God is not. If you feel like you're going through Hell, don't worry. God will not leave you there. Sometimes the path of life is through the gates of "Hell." As you're going through Hell, be sure to leave anything that belongs to Hell right there. As you come out of this circumstance, leave fear, pain, and insecurities behind. Ask God to show you anything in your soul that belongs in Hell. Write your thoughts here.

_____

_____

_____

Give the gift of your presence. Share the joy of God in you. Put down your phone and give someone your undivided attention. Listen to understand their thoughts, desires, and feelings.

Day 6

Drive Your Mind

Romans 8:5 For they that are after the flesh do mind the things of the flesh; but they that are after the Spirit the things of the Spirit. **6**For to be carnally minded is death; but to be spiritually minded is life and peace.

What are you after? Your desires will drive your mind, and your mind will drive you to life or to death, to greater joy or deeper depression. Driving your mind is beyond the power of positive thinking. It involves taking your brain off autopilot. Meditate on what you want, or even better, what you *want* to want. "God help me want what is right." Write your thoughts.

_____

_____

_____

_____

Give the gift of mindfulness. Send someone a note of kindness, just because you were thinking good thoughts about them. Be sure and mention the details of those good thoughts.

Day 7

Relationship Capital

John 16:23 Until now you have not asked [The Father] for anything in My name; but now ask and keep on asking and you will receive, so that your joy may be full and complete.

Coach Anna McCoy teaches the value of "relationship capital." The people in your life are a part of your wealth. Jesus introduced this concept to His disciples when He told them to ask and receive from their Heavenly Father based on His character and reputation, not their own. Have you been feeling like you don't deserve the things that bring you joy? Meditate on the character of Jesus; is there is anything God would withhold from Him? (Psalm 84:11) How will this change your approach to prayer? Write your thoughts here.

Give the gift of relationship. Connect with a potential mentee or mentor. Set a date and keep it.

Day 8
Wild Joy!

Jude 1:24 Now to Him who is able to keep you from stumbling or falling into sin, and to present you unblemished [blameless and faultless] in the presence of His glory with triumphant joy and unspeakable delight, 25 to the only God our Savior, through Jesus Christ our Lord, be glory, majesty, dominion, and power, before all time and now and forever. Amen.

God has called us to live a powerful life, free from bondage to sin. What's more, He is committed to keeping us free. The joy in Jude 1:24 is described as "wild joy," and it comes from living free from the slavery of sin. God issues the command "Be Ye Holy" not to deny you the pleasure of sin, but to bring you into the *wild* joy of freedom from sin. Meditate on that freedom, receive that joy, and write your thoughts here.

_____

 Give the gift of freedom. Do you know someone who is bound by sin? Invite them to a worship service.

Day 9

A Reason to Rejoice

Luke 10:20 Nevertheless do not rejoice at this, that the spirits are subject to you, but rejoice that your names are recorded in heaven."

When the disciples returned from a ministry trip amazed at the power they demonstrated over all the power of the enemy, Jesus put their priorities in place. Yes, believers have the ability to exercise authority, but the greatest joy is in our connection to Heaven. Gifts and authority flow through our relationship with God and our desire to help people. What gifts has the Lord given you? How can you joyfully serve others with them?

_____

_____

_____

_____

 Give the gift of appreciation. Give a compliment or gift to someone who serves their gift well. Tell them why you appreciate them.

Day 10

Set Over Much

Matthew 25:21 His master said to him, 'Well done, good and faithful servant. You have been faithful over a little; I will set you over much. Enter into the joy of your master.

The fear of failure is a powerful joy thief. This fear uses false humility to keep believers in poverty. The parable of the talents speaks of the wicked and lazy servant too afraid to invest what the Master had entrusted in him (Matthew 25:18). But the good and faithful servant took risks, made investments, and did work. The result was more responsibility (and trust from his master) and JOY. Take inventory of the gifts and abilities God has invested in you. How can you use them in a joyful way?

Give the gift of your best self. Invest in something that will make you better. Eat a healthy meal, watch a TED talk, read a blog in your field, get some exercise, or go to bed early.

Day 11

Enduring Joy

James 1:2 Consider it nothing but joy, my [a]brothers and sisters, whenever you fall into various trials. **3** Be assured that the testing of your faith [through experience] produces endurance [leading to spiritual maturity, and inner peace].

What's tempting you? Be assured, Jesus did not lead you into it. If you've faced this temptation or trial before and caved in, you have another opportunity to build your endurance and win! Write down the qualities of the type of person who successfully overcomes the type of trial you are facing. Rejoice, God is building that in you.

_____

_____

_____

Give the gift of endurance. Show support, confidence and hope in someone in your world and help them endure.

Day 12

Morning Joy

Psalm 30:5 For his anger is but for a moment, and his favor is for a lifetime. Weeping may tarry for the night, but joy comes with the morning.

Can you remember something you cried about in the past? How did God heal your emotions and restore your joy? You are stronger than you think. Is there something heavy on your heart today? Measure that thing against the bigness of God. Search the scriptures and write down God's promise for your situation.

_____

_____

_____

_____

_____

30 DAYS OF JOYFUL MEDITATION

Give the gift of a good morning. Buy someone a cup of coffee and wish them a great day.

Day 13

Healed, Delivered and Set Free

Act 8:7 For unclean spirits, crying out with a loud voice, came out of many who had them, and many who were paralyzed or lame were healed. **8** So there was much joy in that city.

Jesus gave us authority over all of the power of the enemy. Exercising that authority brings much joy! Write down some things from which God has delivered or healed you. What is possible now because of that freedom? Not quite free yet? List your motivation for wanting to be free. "I want to be free from _____ so I can _____."

_____
_____
_____
_____

30 DAYS OF JOYFUL MEDITATION

Give the gift of a healing. Donate to the American Cancer Society or your favorite disease fighting charity. Check www.guidestar.org for a comprehensive list.

Day 14

Dig Another Well

Genesis 26:22 He moved away from there and dug another well, and they did not quarrel over that one; so he named it Rehoboth (broad places), saying, "For now the Lord has made room for us, and we shall be prosperous in the land."

Maintaining your joy requires that you say "no" to useless quarrels with selfish people. This was the third well Isaac and his servants dug. The other two were named "quarreling" and "enmity" because the Philistines fought with him saying, "The water is ours." Isaac wanted water not war, so he trusted God to make room for his prosperity and God did exactly that. How can you keep your focus the next time you're tempted to engage in a senseless argument with a selfish person? How can you maintain your focus if you need to dig another well?

30 DAYS OF JOYFUL MEDITATION

Give the gift of a peace. Have a day free from arguments or any form of strife. Hint: Strife is about who is right. Conflict is about what is right.

Day 15

Abounding Joy

Psalm 4:7 You have put more joy in my heart than they have when their grain and wine abound.

We have all felt heartache when a beloved celebrity commits suicide. It's hard to imagine that someone so successful would feel so hopeless. But hopelessness happens when the things we think will make us happy, like money and success, don't make us genuinely happy. Only the Kingdom of God can produce real joy. Meditate on the value of God's joy.

Give the gift of a hope. Tell someone who is highly gifted or successful what you love and appreciate about them specifically and say nothing about their gift or talent.

Day 16

Always be Joyful

 **1 Thessalonians 5:16** Always be joyful.

 How can you always be joyful? Practice emotional awareness. Examine your feelings right now. How are you feeling and why? Is there anything that needs to be adjusted? Ask God for help.

Give the gift of a listening. Ask a friend, "How do you feel?" Practice active listening. Prove it with a follow-up question.

Day 17

Shouts of Joy

Proverbs 11:10 When it goes well for the righteous, the city rejoices And when the wicked perish, there are shouts of joy.

God's plan to promote you is a part of His larger plan to bless others. What good would you like to do? Think beyond your family needs and think about bringing the Kingdom to the world around you. How could our world be better as a result of God prospering you? Write your answers.

_____

_____

_____

_____

_____

_____

30 DAYS OF JOYFUL MEDITATION

Give the gift of prosperity. Sow a financial seed into someone who has made your world better. Tell them HOW their success had changed you.

Day 18

Our Daily Joy

Acts 2:46 Day after day they met in the temple [area] continuing with one mind, and breaking bread in various private homes. They were eating their meals together with joy and generous hearts.

Joy is found in what you do every day. The members of the first church met at the temple daily and hosted dinner parties regularly as a part of their devotion to God. Is there something you can do each day that brings you joy? That perfect cup of coffee or tea, a generous belly laugh, or just a moment of peace and quiet? Maintaining your joy is a part of your devotion to God. Write down at least three simple but impactful things you can do to maintain your joy routinely.

30 DAYS OF JOYFUL MEDITATION

Give the gift of a meal. Treat a friend or family member to a meal at a restaurant or at your home. Discover and discuss something you both love.

Day 19

Lost in Translation

John 15:18-19 (msg) "If you find the godless world is hating you, remember it got its start hating me. If you lived on the world's terms, the world would love you as one of its own. But since I picked you to live on God's terms and no longer on the world's terms, the world is going to hate you.

Have you ever been annoyed by people speaking a foreign language in your presence? Your Force of Joy can have that same effect on people who don't have what you have. Misery loves company and those around you may feel offended if you don't partake in their gloom. Who is most likely to be annoyed with your joyful life? How will you maintain your joy in their presence and not let your joy get lost in translation?

Give the gift of diversity. Do have a bilingual friend? Ask them to teach you a greeting or two. If not, there's always Google!

Day 20

Work with Joy

Ecclesiastes 3:12 I know that there is nothing better for them than to rejoice and to do good as long as they live; **13** and also that every man should eat and drink and see *and* enjoy the good of all his labor—it is the gift of God.

Even if you're not in your dream job yet, your work is still a gift from God and you can "see and enjoy the good" in it. Our work-life allows us to demonstrate the character of God. Excellence, integrity, and professionalism are all developed in the workplace—not to mention the financial resources. Write down three reasons why you are thankful for your job and ask God to help you give Him glory in it?

_____

_____

_____

Give the gift of excellence. Email your employer and thank him/her for your job. Mention one thing about your work that you truly enjoy.

Day 21

Control + "S"

2 Timothy 4:16 At my first trial no one supported me [as an advocate] *or* stood with me, but they all deserted me. May it not be counted against them [by God]. **17** But the Lord stood by me and strengthened *and* empowered me, so that through me the [gospel] message might be fully proclaimed, and that all the Gentiles might hear it; and I was rescued from the [d]mouth of the lion. **18** The Lord will rescue me from every evil assault, and He will bring me safely into His heavenly kingdom; to Him be the glory forever and ever. Amen.

Emotion creates memory like pressing "control + S" on your computer. You can save the portion you want to recall and create a mental file to open again and again. Look at how the Apostle Paul shares a memory with Timothy. Verses 16 and 17 are both true.

Verse 18 however, is a future sentence. The content of verse 18 is determined by which of the previous verses has the greater weight in Paul's mind. How do you see your future—supported by God or deserted by men? Recall a time when people disappointed you, but God supported you. Highlight the right things.

_____
_____
_____
_____
_____
_____
_____
_____
_____
_____

Give the gift of support. Send a "just checking on you" to someone who is going through a tough season. Allow them to update you on their progress. God may use you to highlight the right things.

Day 22

No Matter What

Psalm 34:1 (TLB) I will praise the Lord no matter what happens. I will constantly speak of his glories and grace. [a] **2** I will boast of all his kindness to me. Let all who are discouraged take heart. **3** Let us praise the Lord together and exalt his name.

It may seem impossible, but no matter what is happening in your life, you can choose what comes out of your mouth in the moment. When you step into a situation that doesn't look or feel good, don't say anything that God is not saying. Write down a situation in which you can practice this strategy until it becomes your natural response.

_____

_____

_____

Give the gift of a testimony. Tell someone or the whole world via social media, about ONE time the Lord showed friendship, generosity, or consideration to you.

Day 23

Son of Encouragement

Acts 4:36 Now Joseph, a Levite and native of Cyprus, who was surnamed Barnabas by the apostles (which translated means Son of Encouragement.

Many people in the early church sold land and brought an offering. However, Barnabas was such an encourager, he became a prominent figure in the book of Acts. (9:27; 11:22-30; 13:1-14:28, etc.) God sends joy-givers to people and places in need of strength. Meditate on the people or places who need YOU. Write your thoughts.

_____

_____

_____

_____

30 DAYS OF JOYFUL MEDITATION

Give the gift of an encouraging word. Point out someone's potential and challenge them to succeed in something specifically related to that potential. Offer any guidance on *how* they can succeed.

Day 24

Set Your Mind

Mark 8:33 But turning around [with His back to Peter] and seeing His disciples, He rebuked Peter, saying, "Get behind Me, Satan; for your mind is not set on God's will or His values and purposes, but on what pleases man."

Sometimes the good plan of God seems like a bad plan for us. Don't panic! Keep your joy by asking, "How could God work this for my good and the good of others?" Is there a situation that comes to mind? How could God make it good?

_____

_____

_____

_____

Give the gift of honesty. Offer a different point of view to someone you may disagree with. Keep your heart set on what is good for them or the cause you're discussing.

Day 25

From Labor to Joy

John 16:21 A woman giving birth to a child has pain because her time has come; but when her baby is born she forgets the anguish because of her joy that a child is born into the world. **22** So with you: Now is your time of grief, but I will see you again and you will rejoice, and no one will take away your joy.

Only fools love pain. But the wise use pain, pushing from labor to reward. Have you been avoiding a necessary pain? If so, you could be delaying the joy you deserve. Meditate until you motivate yourself. What will you do first? When will you do it? What will be the reward?

_____

_____

_____

_____

Give the gift of respect. Generously tip to a server or someone who works for you, like your mail carrier, gardener, or stylist. Mention something they do that you appreciate.

Day 26

Reconciled to Joy

Gen 33:4 But Esau ran to meet him and embraced him, and hugged his neck and kissed him, and they wept [for joy].

Reconciliation brings joy. Esau's brother expected him to have a grudge against him. Instead, Esau met Jacob with great JOY. Is there a family member or friend who has wronged you? How has God blessed you in spite of what they did? Ask God to show you how to let it go.

Give the gift of grace. Show grace to someone today by forgiving their bad behavior. Allow God to recompense you rather than hold a grudge.

Day 27

Sold Out to Joy

Matthew 13:44 "The kingdom of heaven is like a [very precious] treasure hidden in a field, which a man found and hid again; then in his joy he goes and sells all he has and buys that field [securing the treasure for himself].

Living joyfully will cost you. For example, you will have to give up your right to complain, sulk, or play the victim. What mental or verbal habits will you have to sacrifice to live a life of joy? Are you ready to sell out for the Kingdom of JOY? Who can help hold you accountable to this commitment?

_____

_____

_____

_____

30 DAYS OF JOYFUL MEDITATION

Give the gift of admission. Help someone pay their way through a toll booth, movie theatre, mission trip, or vacation. Make a recommendation for someone.

Day 28

A Joyful Future

Romans 15:13 May the God of hope fill you with all joy and peace in believing, so that by the power of the Holy Spirit you may abound in hope.

It's impossible to have God and have no picture of our future. He is the God of hope. Imagine your life one year from today; a year of greater energy, focus and health. What good would have happened as result of joyful living?

_____

_____

_____

_____

_____

Give the gift of a future. Is there someone you plan to have around for a long time? Tell them so and tell them why.

Day 29

Joy MD

Provers 17:22 A happy heart is good medicine *and* a joyful mind causes healing, But a broken spirit dries up the bones.

Laughter is a workout for the entire body. It releases endorphins that reduce stress and lower blood pressure. Why do you think the Lord designed your body to respond that way to laughter? How will you bring more laughter into your life today?

_____

_____

_____

_____

_____

_____

_____

Give the gift of laughter. Share a joke—good or bad and the loudest belly laugh you've got!

Day 30

Forever Joyful

Isaiah 40:31 But those who wait for the Lord [who expect, look for, and hope in Him] Will gain new strength and renew their power; They will lift up their wings [and rise up close to God] like eagles [rising toward the sun]; They will run and not become weary, They will walk and not grow tired.

.

Have you ever won a lifetime supply of anything? You have a lifetime supply of JOY, redeemable in the presence of God. Remember, it's not your joy. It's HIS joy bubbling up in you whenever you need it. Meditate on why God is joyful and how you can connect to that joy.

_____

_____

_____

30 DAYS OF JOYFUL MEDITATION

_____
_____
_____
_____
_____
_____
_____
_____
_____
_____
_____
_____
_____
_____
_____
_____
_____
_____
_____
_____

 Give the gift of a JOY. Send a thank you gift to the person who prayed for you on day one of this joyful journey. Celebrate!!

ABOUT THE AUTHOR

Pam Ross is an Inspirer with a powerful ability to identify and activate the genius in others. She is a multiplier who has led hundreds of teams and thousands of individuals to dramatically increase their personal leadership and team-building ability.

"Our greatest wealth is found in people who are willing to discover and embrace who they really are."

Pam uses all forms of media to reach a global audience with her dynamic message of serving, leading and loving. Pam is the president and lead trainer of Kingdom Leadership Development, a non-profit training and consulting organization. She is also chief of staff and associate pastor at All Nations Worship Assembly, Chicago. Pam is the mother of three adult daughters, Imani, Nia and Zoe.

Visit PamRoss.com for other books and resources by Pam Ross

Made in the USA
Coppell, TX
27 December 2020